First World War
and Army of Occupation
War Diary
France, Belgium and Germany

2 DIVISION
3 Light Brigade
Rifle Brigade (The Prince Consort's Own)
53 Battalion
21 March 1919 - 21 October 1919

WO95/1374/12

The Naval & Military Press Ltd
www.nmarchive.com
Published in association with The National Archives

Published by

The Naval & Military Press Ltd

Unit 10 Ridgewood Industrial Park,

Uckfield, East Sussex,

TN22 5QE England

Tel: +44 (0) 1825 749494

www.naval-military-press.com

www.nmarchive.com

This diary has been reprinted in facsimile from the original. Any imperfections are inevitably reproduced and the quality may fall short of modern type and cartographic standards.

© **Crown Copyright**
Images reproduced by permission of The National Archives, London, England, 2015.

Contents

Document type	Place/Title	Date From	Date To
Heading	WO95/1374/12		
Heading	2 Division 3 Light Brigade 53 Bn The Rifle Bde 1919 Mar-1919 Oct		
War Diary	Tilbury	21/03/1919	21/03/1919
War Diary	At Sea	22/03/1919	22/03/1919
War Diary	Antwerp	23/03/1919	25/03/1919
War Diary	Enroute	26/03/1919	27/03/1919
War Diary	Derichsweiler & Schlich	28/03/1919	08/04/1919
War Diary	Bedburg	09/04/1919	15/07/1919
War Diary	Benrath	16/07/1919	21/10/1919

WO 95/13744/2

~~LIGHT~~ 2 DIVISION

3 LIGHT BRIGADE

53 BN THE RIFLE BDE

1919 MAR — 1919 OCT

Army Form C. 2118

WAR DIARY
or
INTELLIGENCE SUMMARY
(Erase heading not required.)

Instructions regarding War Diaries and Intelligence Summaries are contained in F. S. Regs., Part II. and the Staff Manual respectively. Title Pages will be prepared in manuscript.

Place	Date	Hour	Summary of Events and Information	Remarks and references to Appendices
Tilbury At Sea.	21/3/19 22/3/19	1600 to 1800	At Battalion embarked on H.M.T. "Sicilian" for Antwerp. Weather cold and dull at sea all day. Concert on board at 2000 hours.	
Antwerp	23/3/19	1100	Battalion disembarked at ANTWERP Docks, and marched to Rest Camp. Weather cold and bright.	
	24/3/19 25/3/19		At the Rest Camp. All ranks given leave to the Town. Rest Camp very comfortable and convenient. Orders received to entrain on 26/3/19.	
En route	26/3/19	1000	Battalion entrained at ANTWERP Docks. Train journey via LIERRE, HASSELT, TONGRES, VISE, MUNSEN, AIX LA CHAPELLE to DUREN, near COLOGNE. All ranks travelled in closed freight trucks, each fitted with a stove. Halts were made at Hasselt and Munsen for meals. Excellent organization at both stations. Men were given bully beef, bread, jam, margarine and tea. At the latter station the Battn. was fed in 15 minutes, in spite of the late hour and complete darkness.	
	27/3/19	0030.	Battalion arrived at DUREN, but remained in the train until 0700 hours. Detrained at 0700 hours and marched to billets, Headquarters, Nos. 2 and 3 Companies at DERICHSWEILER, and Nos. 1 & 4 Companies at SCHLICH. The day was spent in allotting billets, taking over transport, cookers, etc., and general organization, and cleaning up. The Battn. is taken on the strength of the 6th (Light) Infantry Brigade, 2nd (Light) Division, IV Corps - Brigade Headquarters, SCHLOSS MERODE, 2nd Division and IV Corps Headquarters at DUREN.	
Derichsweiler + Schlich	28/3/19 29/3/19.		Day spent in cleaning up and organization. " " " " " " and short parade.	

- 1 -

Army Form C. 2118

WAR DIARY
or
INTELLIGENCE SUMMARY

(Erase heading not required.)

Instructions regarding War Diaries and Intelligence Summaries are contained in F. S. Regs., Part II. and the Staff Manual respectively. Title Pages will be prepared in manuscript.

Place	Date	Hour	Summary of Events and Information	Remarks and references to Appendices
Derichsweiler + Schlich	30/3/19		Day spent resting the men. Battalion paid at 1500 hours. Regimental Institute and Canteen opened. Concert at Derichsweiler at 2000 organised by Lieut. C.D. Piper.	
	31/3/19		Parades and inspections. Regular training resumed. Lewis Gun and Signalling classes resumed.	

F. Lofts, A/Capt. fr
LIEUT.-COLONEL,
Commdg. 58nd Battn. Rifle Brigade.

Army Form C. 2118.

WAR DIARY
or
INTELLIGENCE SUMMARY.
(Erase heading not required.)

53rd R.B.

Place	Date	Hour	Summary of Events and Information	Remarks and references to Appendices
Deriescweiler	1/4/19		Training as usual. Weather bad, cold and wet.	Appx.
Schub.	2/4/19		Training as usual. Inspection of the Battn. at training by Lieut. General Sir I.J. MORIN, K.C.B., K.C.M.G., Commanding IV Corps.	Appx.
	3/4/19		Battn. route march to WEITZ and back via GITCH and BERGEICH returning at 1500 hours. Inter Company football match in the afternoon. Weather fine.	Appx.
	4/4/19		Battn. marched to DUREN by Companies to the baths. The baths closed in the afternoon in consequence of a breakdown of the machinery. Battn. paid. Ten officers joined the Battn. from cadres of other Battns. of the Rifle Brigade.	Appx.
	5/4/19		Two Companies bathed at DUREN. Weather fine.	Appx.
	6/4/19		Church parade for Headquarters (Company at Battn. Headquarters. Two Companies marched to DUREN for bathing. Brigade is re-designated the 3rd Light Brigade, commanded by Brigadier General H.P.B.L. KENNEDY, C.M.G., D.S.O., V.M.S.O., and consist of 51st, 52nd and 53rd Battns. RIFLE BRIGADE.	Appx.
	7/4/19		Preparations being made for move of the Battn. to BEDBURG - day spent in packing and transporting to DUREN station.	Appx.
	8/4/19		Reveille 0430 hours. Battn. paraded at 0600 hours to march to the entraining station, DUREN. Entrained 0900 hours and left DUREN at 1000 hours, arriving at BEDBURG at 1030 hours. Marched to billets and the rest of the day spent in cleaning billets and arranging offices, etc. Battn. very comfortably accommodated. Regimental Canteen opened the same day.	Appx.
Bedburg.	9/4/19		Day spent in clearing up, packing away stores, arranging offices and allotting billets. Headquarters and Nos. 2 and 4 Companies billeted in the Rheinische Wohlsammwerke Dry's Factory. Very comfortably and airy accommodation for the men. Battn. Headquarters offices accommodated in the factory offices over convenient quarters.	Appx.

Army Form C. 2118.

WAR DIARY
or
INTELLIGENCE SUMMARY.
(Erase heading not required.)

Instructions regarding War Diaries and Intelligence Summaries are contained in F. S. Regs., Part II. and the Staff Manual respectively. Title pages will be prepared in manuscript.

Place	Date	Hour	Summary of Events and Information	Remarks and references to Appendices
Bedburg.	10/4/19.		Training resumed. The G.O.C. 2nd Division inspected the Battn. billets and offices.	SS/1
	11/4/19.		Training as usual. Battn. paid. Weather wet.	SS/1
	12/4/19.		One of the large factory buildings opened as a Battn. Mess Room, accommodating the entire Battn. Football match in the afternoon v. 51st Battn. Rifle Brigade: result: 23rd R.B. 1 - 51st R.B. Nil. Weather wet.	SS/1
	13/4/19.		Church Parade cancelled on account of wet. A fire occurred in the Linoleum Factory at 1240 in the loft adjoining the transport stables of the First Rifle Brigade. Fire picquet turned out very promptly and the fire was got under with the aid of the factory fire appliances.	SS/1
			Capt. J.A. Grawthon and Lieut. W. Barlow proceeded to England for demobilisation.	
	14/4/19.		Major Macphail placed in charge of a Battn. Fire Brigade, and commenced training immediately. Lieut. Colonel W.W. Seymour took over command of the Battn. and Lieut. Colonel The Hon. N.G. Gathorne-Hardy, D.S.O. took over 2nd in Command.	SS/1
	15/4/19.		Training as usual. New Regimental Canteen opened in a vacant shop near Battn. Headquarters.	SS/1
	16/4/19.		2nd Inspection by Brigadier General H.W.F.L. KINNEDY, C.M.G., D.S.O., Commanding 2nd Rifle Brigade. Weather wet.	SS/1
	17/4/19.		Training as usual.	SS/1
	18/4/19.		Good Friday. Voluntary Church Service at 1000 hours. Weather fine. No parades.	SS/1

WAR DIARY
or
INTELLIGENCE SUMMARY.
(Erase heading not required.)

Army Form C. 2118.

Place	Date	Hour	Summary of Events and Information	Remarks and references to Appendices
Bedburg	19/4/19		Football match against 51st Rifle Brigade; result, 53rd R.B. 2 goals 51st R.B. Nil. Concert in the evening.	Appx 1.
	20/4/19		Church Parade at 1100 hours. Weather fine.	Appx 1.
	21/4/19		Holiday for the Battalion. Football match against Brigade H.Q. Result: 53rd R.B. 4 goals, H.Q. 1 goal. A party of 16 O.R. proceeded to Cologne for a river trip.	Appx 1.
	22/4/19		Inspection by G.O.C. 2nd Light Division at 1100 hours. Weather fine.	Appx 1.
	23/4/19		Rugby match against 52nd Rifle Brigade. 53rd Battn. R.B. lost. Regimental baths opened in Linoleum Factory. Battn. ~~widrkxxxk~~	Appx 1.
	24/4/19		Battn. route march. Major T. Woombell, MBE. takes over command of No. 2 Coy. Battalion paid out.	Appx 1.
	26/4/19		Captain Langdale-Smith, R.A.M.C., proceeded to England for demobilization. Two cases of measles and 2 of mumps have occurred in the past few days. Football match to have been played against 52nd Rifle Brigade, but weather prevented play.	Appx 1.
	27/4/19		Church parade at 0950 hours. Weather very cold. Football match against 6th Field Ambulance.	Appx 1.
	29/4/19		Concert by Divisional Concert Party at 2000 hours.	Appx 1.
	"		Battalion route march at 0900 hours. Weather fine.	

W. Johnson Havers Major Lieut. Col.
for C
Commanding 53rd Bn. R.B.

Army Form C. 2118.

WAR DIARY
or
INTELLIGENCE SUMMARY.

53 R.B.

(Erase heading not required.)

Instructions regarding War Diaries and Intelligence Summaries are contained in F. S. Regs., Part II. and the Staff Manual respectively. Title pages will be prepared in manuscript.

Place	Date	Hour	Summary of Events and Information	Remarks and references to Appendices
BEDBURG	1/5/19		Companies paid out. Weather very wet.	
	2/5/19		Lecture by Commander Viscount Broome, R.N., on Naval Subjects, at 1400 hours.	
	3/5/19		Football match between Headquarters & No. 1 Coy. resulting in a win for the latter.	
	4/5/19		Two cases of measles reported in No. 1 Coy. Church Parade at 1100 hours. Weather fine.	
	5/5/19		One case of measles in No. 4 Coy. and one case in No. 2 Coy. The whole Battalion now isolated.	
	6/5/19		Inspection by H.R.H. The Duke of Connaught (Colonel,-in-Chief) Weather fine.	
	7/5/19		Football match between 51st and 53rd R.B.; result 51st 1, 53rd nil. Battalion route march.	
	8/5/19		Lecture at 1030 hours in Y.M.C.A. on Reconstruction by Canon Mayrick.	
	9/5/19		Companies paid out. Weather very hot.	
	10/5/19		Work commenced at new camp for Nos. 1 and 2 Companies. Weather very stormy.	
	11/5/19		Church Parade at 1000. Football match, Officers v. Sergts, resulting in win for Officers.	
	12/5/19		Company training as usual. Heavy thunderstorm.	
	13/5/19		Quarterly inspection of rifles.	
	14/5/19		Battalion route march, weather very hot. Tents for new camp arrive.	
	15/5/19		Nos. 1 and 2 Companies move under canvas just outside Bedburg.	
	16/5/19		Companies paid out. Weather very hot.	

Army Form C. 2118.

WAR DIARY
or
INTELLIGENCE SUMMARY.
(Erase heading not required.)

Instructions regarding War Diaries and Intelligence Summaries are contained in F. S. Regs., Part II. and the Staff Manual respectively. Title pages will be prepared in manuscript.

Place	Date	Hour	Summary of Events and Information	Remarks and references to Appendices
BIHR-Ra	17/5/19		Lecture by Mr. Sandon Perkins, Y.M.C.S. Subject, "Midst Arctic Snows," in Y.M.C.A. at 1100 hours.	1085
	18/5/19		Church parade at 1100 hours in Y.M.C.A.	1085
	19/5/19		Company training as usual. Weather very hot.	1085
	20/5/19		One case of measles from Orderly Room Staff.	1085
	21/5/19		Concert by "Starlights" (Light Division) Concert Party in Regimental Theatre at 2000 hours. Battn. route march.	1085
	22/5/19		Divisional Cinema visited the Battn. and gave show at 2000 hours. Cricket match, H.Q. Coy. v No. 3 Coy. H.Q. won by 25 runs.	1085
	23/5/19		Companies paid out.	1085
	24/5/19		Holiday for Battn., being Empire Day. Battn. sports held at 1400 hours.	1085
	25/5/19		Brigade Church Parade 1000 hours. Warning Order re probable move received from Brigade.	1085
	26/5/19		Football match between H.Q. and No. 3 Coy. Result, No. 3 Coy. 1 H.Q. 0.	1085
	27/5/19		Cricket match at 1430 hours between No. 1 Coy and No. 2 Coy. No. 2 Coy. won by 34 runs. Cricket match between Officers and Sergeants at 1730 hours. Officers won by 2 runs.	1085
	28/5/19		Training as usual.	1085
	29/5/19		Inspection by Commander-in-Chief. Companies paid out. Football match against 1st Dragoons, who won 2-0.	1085
	30/5/19		Divisional General Inspected cooking, sanitary arrangements, etc.	1085

Army Form C. 2118.

WAR DIARY
or
INTELLIGENCE SUMMARY.
(Erase heading not required.)

Instructions regarding War Diaries and Intelligence Summaries are contained in F. S. Regs., Part II. and the Staff Manual respectively. Title pages will be prepared in manuscript.

Place	Date	Hour	Summary of Events and Information	Remarks and references to Appendices
	31/5/19		Battn. route march. Cricket match, Officers v. Sergts. Result, Sergts. won by 61 runs.	

W. W. Seymour,
Lieut. Colonel,
Commanding 53rd Battn. THE RIFLE BRIGADE.

Army Form C. 2118

WAR DIARY
or
INTELLIGENCE SUMMARY

(Erase heading not required.)

Instructions regarding War Diaries and Intelligence Summaries are contained in F.S. Regs., Part II. and the Staff Manual respectively. Title Pages will be prepared in manuscript.

53rd R Bn
June 1919

Place	Date	Hour	Summary of Events and Information	Remarks and references to Appendices
BEDBURG	1/6/19.		Brigade Parade at 1015 hrs. Cricket match between Headquarters and No. 3 Company. Headquarters won by 1 run.	
	2/6/19.		Preparations commenced for Nos. 3 and 4 Companies and Headquarters to move under canvas with Nos. 1 and 2 Companies. 50 bell tents arrive.	
	3/6/19.		Being Birthday of H.M. The King, Brigade paraded at 1000 hours on 51st Bn. The Rifle Brigade Football Ground, when the Royal Salute was given. The remainder of the day observed as a holiday. Sports were to have been held but were cancelled owing to bad weather.	
	4/6/19.		Sports were held at 1500 hours.	
	5/6/19.		Cross-country run at 0730 hours. Battalion paid out.	
	6/6/19.		Tents arrive and are put up ready for Nos. 3 and 4 Companies and Headquarters to move into Camp.	
	7/6/19.		Nos. 3 and 4 Companies and Headquarters move into Camp.	
	8/6/19.		Church parade at 1000 hours. 51st Battn. Sports.	
	9/6/19.		Holiday for Battn. 52nd Bn. Sports held at KONIGSHOVEN.	
	10/6/19.		First day of Boxing Tournament: a great success.	
	11/6/19.		Battn. route march at 0800 hours. 18 O.R.s proceeded to England for leave prior to joining a Regular unit. Second and last day of Boxing Tournament. Divisional General and Staff present.	
	12/6/19.		Company training as usual. Very violent storm at 1600 hours. Xompanies paid out.	
	13/6/19.		Corps Commander visited the Battn. to inspect Institutes.	

- 1 -

Army Form C. 2118

WAR DIARY
or
INTELLIGENCE SUMMARY
(Erase heading not required.)

Instructions regarding War Diaries and Intelligence Summaries are contained in F.S. Regs., Part II. and the Staff Manual respectively. Title Pages will be prepared in manuscript.

Place	Date	Hour	Summary of Events and Information	Remarks and references to Appendices
BEDBURG	14/6/19.			
	15/6/19.		Brigade Church Parade at 1100 hours.	
	16/6/19.		Cricket match between No. 2 and No. 4 Company, resulting in a win for No. 2 Coy.	
	17/6/19.		Orders received to proceed by march route to MULHEIM (COLOGNE Area)	
	18/6/19.		Battalion moves by march route to POULHEIM.	
	19/6/19.		" " " " BICKENDORF Area.	
	20/6/19.		" " " " MULHEIM Area Nos. 1 & 4 Companies and Headquarters at MULHEIM, No. 2 Company at DELLBRUCK, No. 3 Company at LEVERKUSEN.	
	21/6/19.		Battalion took over all guards from 18th K.R.R.C.	
	22/6/19.		Church Parade at MULHEIM at 0900 hours.	
	23/6/19.		Companies paid out.	
	24/6/19.		Divisional General inspected all Battalion Guards in MULHEIM Area. Weather very wet.	
	25/6/19.		Companies paid out.	
	26/6/19.		Nos 4 Company relieved No. 3 Company at LEVERKUSEN, No. 3 Company coming to MULHEIM.	
	27/6/19.		No. 1 Company relieved No. 2 Company at DELLBRUCK, No. 2 Company coming into MULHEIM.	
	28/6/19.		Peace signed. 53rd Battn. The Rifle Brigade, the junior Battn. of the Regiment, the only Battn. The Rifle Brigade to cross the Rhine.	

- 2 -

Army Form C. 2118

WAR DIARY
or
INTELLIGENCE SUMMARY
(Erase heading not required.)

Instructions regarding War Diaries and Intelligence Summaries are contained in F. S. Regs., Part II. and the Staff Manual respectively. Title Pages will be prepared in manuscript.

Place	Date	Hour	Summary of Events and Information	Remarks and references to Appendices
BEDBURG	29/6/19		Church Parade at 0900 hours. Warning order received to Return to BEDBURG.	
	30/6/19.		Transport completed first party of journey to BEDBURG.	

BEDBURG.
3/7/19.

ORDERLY ROOM
No...
4 JUL 1919
53rd BATTN. RIFLE BRIGADE

E. Unknown, Maj.
for Lieut. Colonel,
Commanding 53rd Battn. THE RIFLE BRIGADE.

Army Form C. 2118

WAR DIARY
or
INTELLIGENCE SUMMARY
(Erase heading not required.)

Instructions regarding War Diaries and Intelligence Summaries are contained in F.S. Regs., Part II. and the Staff Manual respectively. Title Pages will be prepared in manuscript.

Place	Date	Hour	Summary of Events and Information	Remarks and references to Appendices
BEDBURG	1/7/19		Training as usual.	
	2/7/19		do. do.	
	3/7/19.		Companies paid out.	
	4/7/19.		Nos. 1 & 2 Companies firing on the Range at MORKEN. Warning Order received re Battn. moving to BENRATH-HILDEN Area. on Monday 7th inst.	
	5/7/19.		Nos. 3 & 4 Companies firing on the Range at MORKEN. Instructions received that move is postponed 24 hours.	
	6/7/19.		Preparations made to move to BENRATH-HILDEN Area.	
	7/7/19.		Advance Party sent to BENRATH. Advance Party arrives from BENRATH. No. 3 Company proceeded to HIMMELGEIST by lorry and took over Nos. 7 & 8 Posts from 8th Bn. Scottish Rifles. No.7 Post being the left Post on the Perimeter, No.8 Post at the Patrol Works Reisholz.	
	8/7/19.		The rest of the Battalion moved by rail to BENRATH, leaving BEDBURG at 0830 hours and relieved 9th Bn. Scottish Rifles at BENRATH on the left of the British Front.	
	9/7/19.		No. 4 Company moved to Petrol Works at REISHOLZ, and relieved 2 Platoons of No. 3 Company, Two Platoons then moved to Himmelgeist.	
	10/7/19.		Companies paid out.	
	11/7/19.		Nos. 1 & 2 Companies training as usual.	
	13/7/19.		Brigade Church Parade at 1100 hours.	
	14/7/19.		No. 2 Company and Headquarters firing on Range at URDENBACH.	
	15/7/19.		No. 1 Company and remainder of Headquarters firing on Range at URDENBACH.	

- 1 -

Army Form C. 2118

WAR DIARY
or
INTELLIGENCE SUMMARY
(Erase heading not required.)

Instructions regarding War Diaries and Intelligence Summaries are contained in F.S. Regs., Part II. and the Staff Manual respectively. Title Pages will be prepared in manuscript.

Place	Date	Hour	Summary of Events and Information	Remarks and references to Appendices
BENRATH	16/7/19		Route march H.Q., Nos. 1 & 2 Companies.	
	17/7/19.		Nos. 1 & 2 Companies & H.Q. training as usual. Cricket match between No. 1 Coy. & H.Q.; H.Q. won easily. Concert in Scottish Church Hut at 2000 hours.	
	18/7/19.		Companies paid out.	
	19/7/19.		Holiday for the Battalion.	
	20/7/19.		Cricket match between the Battn. and Headquarters R.A. Result: Battn. won by an innings & 3 runs.	
	21/7/19.		Training as usual. Weather very wet.	
	22/7/19.		do. do.	
	23/7/19.		Holiday for the Battalion. Rifle Meeting arranged, but owing to bad weather had to be postponed. Concert in the evening at 1930 hours in Scottish Churches Hut by the "Maxims" 29th Bn. M.G.C. Concert Party.	
	24/7/19.		No. 1 Company relieved No. 3 Company at HIMMELGEIST. No. 2 Company relieved No. 4 Company at the Petrol Works at REISHOLZ.	
	25/7/19.		Companies paid out. No. 4 Company firing on the Range at URDENBACH.	
	26/7/19.		No. 3 Company firing on the Range at URDENBACH.	
	27/7/19.		Church Parade at 1100 hours at Protestant Church, BENRATH.	
	28/7/19.		Inspection of cook-houses, Transport & Institutes by Brig.-General Commanding 3rd Light Brigade.	
	29/7/19.		Training as usual for Nos. 3, 4 & H.Q. Companies.	

-- 2 --

Army Form C. 2118

WAR DIARY
or
INTELLIGENCE SUMMARY
(Erase heading not required.)

Instructions regarding War Diaries and Intelligence Summaries are contained in F.S. Regs., Part II. and the Staff Manual respectively. Title Pages will be prepared in manuscript.

Place	Date	Hour	Summary of Events and Information	Remarks and references to Appendices
BENRATH	30/7/19.		Cricket match between Battalion and A/246th Battery R.F.A. Result: Bn. won by 2 wickets and 54 runs.	
	31/7/19.		Companies paid out. 10 men proceeded to England for leave prior to Joining a Regular Unit.	
			[signature]	
			Lieut. Colonel,	
			Commanding 3rd Bn. THE RIFLE BRIGADE	
	2/8/19.			

Army Form C. 2118

3rd R.B.

WAR DIARY
or
INTELLIGENCE SUMMARY
(Erase heading not required.)

Instructions regarding War Diaries and Intelligence Summaries are contained in F.S. Regs., Part II. and the Staff Manual respectively. Title Pages will be prepared in manuscript.

Place	Date	Hour	Summary of Events and Information	Remarks and references to Appendices
BENRATH.	1/8/19.		Nos. 3 & 4 Companies and Headquarters training as usual.	
	2/8/19.		Football match between the Battalion and A/246th Batty. R.F.A. Result: draw, 2 goals each.	
	3/8/19.		Church Parade for 3, 4 and Headquarters Companies at 1100 hours.	
	4/8/19.		Holiday for the Battalion. Fishing Competition held. The winners were L/Cpl. Maskell for the heaviest weight of fish and L/Cpl. Stevens for the heaviest fish.	
	5/8/19.		45 all ranks of the Battalion went on Rhine Trip from Cologne to Coblenz.	
	6/8/19.		Nos. 3, 4 & Headquarters Companies training as usual.	
	7/8/19.		Nos. 3, 4 & Headquarters Companies training as usual.	
	8/8/19.		Examination of candidates for 2nd Class Army Certificates at the School Room.	
	9/8/19.		Examination of candidates for 3rd Class Army Certificates at the School Room.	
	10/8/19.		Church Parade for Nos. 3, 4 & Headquarters Companies at 1100 hours.	
	11/8/19.		Nos. 3 & 4 & Headquarters Companies training as usual.	
	12/8/19.		Nos. 1 & 2 Companies were relieved on outpost line by Nos. 3 & 4 Companies.	
	13/8/19.		Nos. 1 & 2 Companies training as usual. Rhine Army Horse Show: 50 O.Ranks granted leave to attend.	
	14/8/19.		Nos. 1 & 2 Companies training as usual.	
	15/8/19.		Companies paid out. War Savings Association opened. First contributions made.	

-- 1 --

Army Form C. 2118

WAR DIARY
or
INTELLIGENCE SUMMARY
(Erase heading not required.)

Instructions regarding War Diaries and Intelligence Summaries are contained in F. S. Regs., Part II. and the Staff Manual respectively. Title Pages will be prepared in manuscript.

Place	Date	Hour	Summary of Events and Information	Remarks and references to Appendices
BENRATH.	16/8/19.		Nos. 1, 2 & Headquarters Companies at disposal of O.Cs for interior economy.	
	17/8/19.		Church Parade for Nos. 1, 2 & Headquarters Companies at 11 00 hours.	
	18/8/19.) 19/8/19.)		Rhine Army Horse Show at Merheim. 50 Other Ranks granted leave to attend.	
	20/8/19.		Rhine Army Acquatic Sports at Cologne. 50 Other Ranks granted leave to attend.	
	21/8/19.) 22/8/19.)		Eliminating Competitions for Divisional Sports. Boxing: out of 5 finals the Battn. won 4.	
	23/8/19.		Nos. 3 & 4 Companies relieved on Outpost line by Nos. 1 & 2 Companies.	
	24/8/19.		Church Parade for Nos. 3 & 4 Companies at 1100 hours.	
	25/8/19.		Regimental Birthday. Day observed as a holiday and devoted to Sports Meeting between 51st, 52nd and 53rd Battalions The Rifle Brigade. The Battalion secured 7 firsts, 6 seconds & 6 third prizes.	
	26/8/19.		Nos. 3, 4 & Headquarters Companies training as usual.	
	27/8/19.		Lieut. Colonel W.W. Seymour proceeded to England and Major M.G.N. Stopford, M.C., 51st Bn. The Rifle Brigade, assumed command.	
	28/8/19.		Nos. 3, 4 & Headquarters Companies training as usual.	
	29/8/19.		From this date Nos. 1, 2, 3 & 4 Companies will be known as "A", "B", "C" & "D" Companies respectively. "C" Company commence their General Musketry Course on Brigade Range at Urdenbach. All leave to United Kingdom for the Light Division is cancelled as from 29th inst. owing to contemplated move.	

Army Form C. 2118

WAR DIARY
or
INTELLIGENCE SUMMARY
(Erase heading not required.)

Instructions regarding War Diaries and Intelligence Summaries are contained in F. S. Regs., Part II. and the Staff Manual respectively. Title Pages will be prepared in manuscript.

Place	Date	Hour	Summary of Events and Information	Remarks and references to Appendices
BENRATH.	30/3/19.		"C" Company continued the G.M.C. "D" Company at the disposal of Company Commander for interior economy. Last Rhine Army Race Meeting.	
	31/3/19.		"C" Company continue to fire their G.M.C. No Church Parade in consequence.	

E.M. Stopford
Major,
Commanding 53rd Battn. THE RIFLE BRIGADE.

BENRATH.
3/9/19.

Army Form C. 2118

3rd R.B.

WAR DIARY
or
INTELLIGENCE SUMMARY
(Erase heading not required.)

Instructions regarding War Diaries and Intelligence Summaries are contained in F.S. Regs., Part II. and the Staff Manual respectively. Title Pages will be prepared in manuscript.

Place	Date	Hour	Summary of Events and Information	Remarks and references to Appendices
BENLAHM	1/9/19.		"C" Company continue to fire their M.M.C.	
	2/9/19.		"B" and "D" Companies continue to fire their M.M.C. "C" Company relieved "A" Company in Outpost line.	
	3/9/19.		"B" Company commenced M.M.C. A concert was given by the Green Jackets Concert Party at the Scottish Churches Hut.	
	4/9/19.		Divisional Sports were held on the Brigade Sports ground commencing at 1400 hours. "A" Company continued to fire M.M.C. "B" Company training as usual.	
	5/9/19.		"A" and "D" Companies continue to fire their M.M.C. Major T. Vosmell, M.B.E., left the Battalion on being posted to the 52nd R. Capt. F.C. Harrison joined as 2nd-in-command of the Battalion.	
	6/9/19.		"A" and "D" Companies continue to fire their M.M.C.	
	7/9/19.		Three Officers and 24 O.R.s left Battalion to proceed to Musketry Office, DHUKE, to represent 3rd Light Brigade at the Rhine Army Rifle Meeting.	
	8/9/19.		"A" and "D" Companies continue to fire their M.M.C. "D" Company completed M.M.C.	
	9/9/19.		"D" Company relieved "L" Company at Army Petrol Installation. "A" Company completed M.M.C.	
	10/9/19.		"B" Company commence to fire their M.M.C. "A" Company training as usual.	
	11/9/19.		"B" Company continue to fire their M.M.C. "A" Company route march.	
	12/9/19.			

- 1 -

Army Form C. 2118

WAR DIARY
or
INTELLIGENCE SUMMARY
(Erase heading not required.)

Instructions regarding War Diaries and Intelligence Summaries are contained in F.S. Regs., Part II. and the Staff Manual respectively. Title Pages will be prepared in manuscript.

Place	Date	Hour	Summary of Events and Information	Remarks and references to Appendices
EN AM	13/9/19.			
	14/9/19.		Football match between HeadQuarters and No. 1 Company, resulting in a draw.	
	15/9/19.		Training as usual for "A" and "B" Companies. Football match between "A" Company and Headquarters.	
	16/9/19.		Concert in Scottish Churches Hut at 1830 hours.	
	17/9/19.		Corps Commander visited the Battalion. Route march for "A" and "B" Companies and Headquarters.	
	18/9/19.		Companies paid out.	
	19/9/19.		Training as usual for "A" and "B" Companies.	
	20/9/19.		Divisional Commander inspected Bttn. Transport Lines and "A" and "B" Companies training. Football match between "A" and "B" Companies : "A" Company won 6-0.	
	21/9/19.		Church Parade for "A" and "B" Companies and Headquarters at 1100 hours.	
	22/9/19.		Relief "A" Company relieved "B" Company at MISSOLZ Patrol Installation. "B" Company relieved "C" Company at NIEMLISZ. "C" Company returned to MERRATH. Divisional Commander inspected "C" Company at MIERAU IST.	
	23/9/19.		Football match between Headquarters and "C" Company. Result: H.Q. 4 "C" Company 0.	
	24/9/19.		Battalion Concert in Scottish Churches Ht at at 2030 hours.	
	25/9/19.		Companies paid out. Training as usual.	

- 2 -

1875 Wt. W593/826 1,000,000 4/15 J.B.C. & A. A.D.S.S./Forms/C. 2118.

Army Form C. 2118

WAR DIARY
or
INTELLIGENCE SUMMARY
(Erase heading not required.)

Instructions regarding War Diaries and Intelligence Summaries are contained in F. S. Regs., Part II. and the Staff Manual respectively. Title Pages will be prepared in manuscript.

Place	Date	Hour	Summary of Events and Information	Remarks and references to Appendices
BENBATH.	26/9/19.		Football match between "C" and "D" Companies employed men and Headquarters. "C" & "D" won.	
	27/9/19.		Training as usual.	
	28/9/19.		Church Parade at 1100 hours.	
	29/9/19.		"D" Company relieved "A" Company at Army Petrol Installation, NIENOLZ. "A" Company returned to BENBATH. "D" Company at NIENBLEISS.	
	30/9/19.		Casuals firing on the Range in the morning, Lewis gunners in the afternoon.	

[signature]

Lieut. Colonel,
Commanding 53rd Bn. THE RIFLE BRIGADE.

BENBATH.
30/9/19.

Army Form C. 2118

WAR DIARY
or
INTELLIGENCE SUMMARY
(Erase heading not required.)

Instructions regarding War Diaries and Intelligence Summaries are contained in F.S. Regs., Part II. and the Staff Manual respectively. Title Pages will be prepared in manuscript.

Place	Date	Hour	Summary of Events and Information	Remarks and references to Appendices
BENRATH.	1/10/19.		Casuals and Lewis Gunners firing on the Range. Football match: Officers v. Sergts. Sergts. won 2 goals to 1.	
	2/10/19.		Casuals and Lewis Gunners firing on the Range. Cross-country run at 1500 hours.	
	3/10/19.		Companies paid out. Casuals and Lewis Gunners firing on the Range.	
	4/10/19.		Casuals and Lewis Gunners finished firing.	
	5/10/19.		Church Parade at 1100 hours in Protestant Church, BENRATH.	
	6/10/19.		Training as usual. Practice Rugby Game at 1430 hours.	
	7/10/19.		"I" Company relieved "A" Company at HIMMELGEIST. "A" Company returned to Army Petrol Installation, REISHOLZ. Soccer match between Battn. and A/245th Battery R.F.A. R.F.A. won 4-0.	
	8/10/19.			
	9/10/19.		Cross-country run at 1430 hours, winner being Lieut. G.D. Piper of "B" Company.	
	10/10/19.		Rugger match v. 41st Bn. M.G.C. M.G.C. won by 12 pts. to 6. Concert in the evening at 1830 hours. "B" and "C" Companies moved to COLOGNE for duty at Rhine Army Munitions Concentration Camp.	
	11/10/19.		"C" Company moved to HIMMELGEIST. Companies paid out. French Officers visited the Battn. area to reconnoitre prior to taking over.	

- 1 -

Army Form C. 2118

WAR DIARY
or
INTELLIGENCE SUMMARY

(Erase heading not required.)

Instructions regarding War Diaries and Intelligence Summaries are contained in F. S. Regs., Part II. and the Staff Manual respectively. Title Pages will be prepared in manuscript.

Place	Date	Hour	Summary of Events and Information	Remarks and references to Appendices
OHLRATH	12/10/19.		Church Parade at 1100 hours.	
	13/10/19.		Battn. prepared to move to OPLADEN on 15th Oct. after being relieved by 171st French Regt.	
	14/10/19.		Orders received cancelling move.	
	15/10/19.		Football match between Transport and H.Q. H.Q. won, 4:3.	
	16/10/19.		Companies paid out.	
	17/10/19.		Lieut. A.R. Gray proceeded to England for demobilisation.	
	18/10/19.		Instructions received re re-organisation of 3rd Light Brigade.	
	19/10/19.		Church Parade at 1100 hours.	
	20/10/19.		Preparations made for "A" and "B" Companies to join 2nd Battn. The Rifle Brigade and "C" and "D" Companies to join 51st Battn. The Rifle Brigade.	
	21/10/19.		Battn. reduced to Cadre strength.	

E.B.Stafford
Lieut. Colonel,
Commanding Cadre, 53rd Bn. THE RIFLE BRIGADE.

OHLRATH, Germany,
22nd Oct. 1919.

www.ingramcontent.com/pod-product-compliance
Lightning Source LLC
Chambersburg PA
CBHW081505160426
43193CB00014B/2593